KENNY JOHNSON

# The Power of a Praying Coach

KLP

KINGDOM LEGACY
PRESS

*To every coach who ever stayed after practice to encourage a player...*
*Whoever went home heavy-hearted, carrying more than a clipboard...*
*Whoever led from a place of love, even when no one saw it...*

*This book is for you.*

*And to the Coach of all coaches —*
*The One who teaches us to serve with humility, lead with courage, and win with wisdom...*

*This book is Yours.*

# Contents

*Preface*                                                               ii

  1   Chapter 1: Why Coaches Must Pray                          1

  2   Chapter 2: Praying for Identity, Integrity,
      and Inner...                                               6

  3   Chapter 3: Praying for Wisdom Under Pressure             12

  4   Chapter 4: Praying for Your Players                      17

  5   Chapter 5: Praying for Team Unity and Chemistry         22

  6   Chapter 9: Praying for Your Career and Calling          27

  7   Chapter 6: Praying Through Wins and Losses              32

  8   Chapter 7: Praying for Parents and Families             36

  9   Chapter 8: Praying for Your Coaching
      Staff and Leadership                                      41

10   Chapter 10: Praying for Your School and Community        46

11   Chapter 11: Praying Against Burnout and
      Spiritual Warfare                                         51

12   Chapter 12: The Lifestyle of a Praying Coach            56

13   Conclusion: The Final Charge                            61

*The Invitation to Salvation*                                           64

# Preface

**The Sacred Name: Yahshua (Jesus)**

Throughout this book, you will notice the name Yahshua (Jesus) used consistently in every prayer, scripture, and spiritual reference. This is not by accident. It is a divine restoration—an invitation to deeper understanding and reverence for the One who came to save.

### 1. Yahshua: The Original Name of the Messiah

Before Greek, Latin, or English translations existed, the Son of God was called by His Hebrew name: Yahshua (עושהי), meaning "Yah is salvation" or "Yahweh saves." This name embodies His mission and identity—not only as Savior but as the fulfillment of the Father's promise.

"She will give birth to a son, and you are to give Him the name Yahshua, because He will save His people from their sins."
   (Matthew 1:21, Hebrew Roots Translation)

In most Bibles, this verse uses the name Jesus, but in the original tongue, Yahshua was the name given. His name connects to the divine name of the Father—Yahweh—revealing the unity between Father and Son.

"I have come in My Father's name, and you do not receive Me."
   (John 5:43)

"Your name, O YHWH, endures forever, Your renown, O YHWH, through all generations."
   (Psalm 135:13)

The very name Yahshua carries that same eternal Name—Yah—which is lost in the Greek and English forms.

### 2. Jesus: The Translated Name with Continued Grace

The name "Jesus" came into popular usage through a series of linguistic transitions:

Hebrew "Yahshua"

Greek "Iēsous" (Greek lacks the "Y" and "sh" sounds)

Latin "Iesus"

English "Jesus" (with the letter "J" being introduced around the 16th century)

Although the name "Jesus" is not linguistically the same as "Yahshua," it carries spiritual power because of the faith and reverence placed in it by generations of believers. God responds to the heart, not merely phonetics.

"There is no other name under heaven given among men by which we must be saved."

(Acts 4:12)

"For whoever calls on the name of the Lord shall be saved."
  (Romans 10:13)

These verses affirm the saving power of the name, even when pronounced differently, so long as the heart is aligned in truth and faith.

### 3. Reclaiming the Power of the Name

In these last days, the Father is restoring lost truths—identities, cultures, and languages that were stripped through colonization, translation, and assimilation. Reclaiming the name Yahshua is not to dismiss or diminish the name "Jesus," but to honor the original and reveal the fullness of His identity.

"The name of YHWH is a strong tower; the righteous run to it and are safe."
  (Proverbs 18:10)

"Then I will restore to the peoples a pure language, that they all may call on the name of YHWH, to serve Him with one accord."
  (Zephaniah 3:9)

The enemy has always sought to distort identity and language, because names carry power, assignment, and spiritual authority. The restoration of Yahshua's name is part of the greater awakening happening among God's people.

### 4. How This Book Will Use His Name

To walk in both truth and accessibility, this book will use Yahshua (Jesus) throughout—bridging the gap between what has been passed down and what is being restored.

"Yahshua the Messiah is the same yesterday, today, and for-ever."
    (Hebrews 13:8, Hebrew Roots Bible)

Every prayer, every scripture, and every reflection is written to honor both the faith many were raised with and the deeper truth now being revealed. Let this understanding open your spirit to greater revelation. May you call on Him, not out of tradition, but with truth and intimacy. Whether you say Jesus or Yahshua, may your prayers be filled with power, and your walk be filled with light.

"And you shall know the truth, and the truth shall make you free."
    (John 8:32)

# 1

# Chapter 1: Why Coaches Must Pray

### *Because Our Voice Is Their Vision*

Coaching is more than a clipboard, a whistle, or a game plan. It's a calling. A sacred assignment. When you coach, you're not just preparing athletes for a game — you're preparing souls for life. And in a world that constantly pulls young people away from truth, identity, and purpose, the role of a coach has never been more critical. And that's why, Coach, you must pray.I didn't always see it this way. Early in my coaching journey, I thought prayer was something I did after a game — to thank God for a win or find peace after a loss. But through trials, burnout, and personal reflection, I realized that prayer isn't a post-game ritual. It's a pre-game requirement: Prayer is preparation. Prayer is power. Prayer is protection.

### *Coaching Without Prayer Is Coaching Without Armor*

The Word says in James 1:8 (NLT): "Their loyalty is divided between God and the world, and they are unstable in everything they do." When I coached without prayer, I was unstable. I led out of stress instead of surrender. I snapped when I should've stayed silent. I tried to carry the weight of it all — the players, the parents, the pressure — without God's help. And it wore me down. It wasn't until I realigned with the Lord that I understood: Coaching is a spiritual battle. And you don't show up to battle without your armor. Ephesians 6:11 (NLT) reminds us: "Put on all of God's armor so that you will be able to stand firm against all strategies of the devil." When you don't pray, you walk into warfare unprotected. But when you do — when you humble yourself and seek the Lord first — you gain wisdom, clarity, patience, and the ability to lead with divine insight, not just human instinct.

### Our Players Don't Just Need Direction. They Need Spiritual Covering.

As coaches, we're one of the most influential voices in our athletes' lives. Some of them don't have fathers at home. Some don't have peace. Some don't know love outside of correction. You are their leader. But also, you're their covering. Just as Moses covered the Israelites in prayer, just as Yahshua (Jesus) intercedes for us even now, you are called to spiritually intercede for the young men and women entrusted to your leadership. "I urge you, first of all, to pray for all people. Ask God to help them; intercede on their behalf, and give thanks for them." — 1 Timothy 2:1 (NLT) Don't just pray for wins. Pray for breakthroughs. Pray for identity. Pray for protection from what they're not even telling you they're going through. I can remember specific players — talented, focused, respectful — but silently hurting. And it wasn't until I began covering them

2

in prayer that I saw the emotional walls come down. The change wasn't just physical or mental — it was spiritual.

### Your Leadership Is a Pulpit, Even Without a Microphone

We may never get on a big stage or behind a pulpit. But our locker room is our church. Our pre-game speech is our sermon. Our interactions are worship. And prayer keeps our leadership aligned with heaven, not ego. As I grew closer to God, I began to shift my perspective. My focus was no longer on stats, record books, or praise. I realized that true success was about how many players I helped lead to the light. What's a trophy if your team doesn't know truth? What's a scholarship if they lose their soul? "And what do you benefit if you gain the whole world but lose your own soul?" — Mark 8:36 (NLT) You can build champions in the gym — but only God builds champions of character. Your role is to partner with Him in that work, and prayer is how you stay connected to the source.

### Scientific Proof: Prayer Makes You a Better Coach

Even the world can't deny it anymore. Harvard Medical School found that daily prayer or meditation lowers cortisol, improves emotional regulation, and enhances decision-making under pressure. Research from the University of Pennsylvania showed that leaders who actively practice spiritual disciplines demonstrate more empathy, higher resilience, and better conflict resolution. Translation? Prayer doesn't just make you holy. It makes you effective.

### My Turning Point

There was a season I led purely from the flesh. I was disciplined, structured, motivational — but spiritually empty. I thought I was doing everything right. But behind the effort was anxiety, burnout, and self-reliance. Then, I surrendered. I made the Word of God my morning playbook. I started praying before practices, games, and team meetings. I even began journaling my prayers for each player by name. What happened? Peace entered. Clarity sharpened. Joy returned. Not because everything got easier — but because I wasn't doing it alone anymore.

### Coaches, This Is Our Mandate

We don't need more motivational quotes. We need more Spirit-led leaders. We need coaches who don't just lead — they cover. Who doesn't just discipline — they disciple. You may be the only godly influence your players encounter this year. Don't waste that moment. Don't wait until it's too late. Pray now. Cover them now. Speak life over them before the world speaks death. "Devote yourselves to prayer with an alert mind and a thankful heart." — Colossians 4:2 (NLT)

### Prayer for the Coach

Heavenly Father,

I surrender my coaching to You. I don't want to lead from stress—I want to lead from Your Spirit. Help me cover my players in prayer, not just with plans. Give me discernment, wisdom, and peace. Let my voice reflect Your love and truth. May every word I speak build life, not ego. Let my example point them to You. In Yahshua's (Jesus') name, Amen.

4

### Reflection & Challenge

Who on your team needs to be covered in prayer by name?

When was the last time you prayed before a practice, not just a game?

This week, start a prayer journal. List your players and write one sentence of blessing or intercession for each.

### Challenge:

Before every game this season, take 5 minutes alone. No phone. No clipboard. Just you and God.

Pray for the game — but more importantly, pray for your growth as a man or woman of God who leads from the inside out.

# 2

# Chapter 2: Praying for Identity, Integrity, and Inner Strength

### *Because Who You Are Is Greater Than What You Do*

As a coach, you're more than your record. You're more than your resume. You're more than how many championships you've won or how many players you've sent to college. Your true influence isn't in the game you teach — it's in the identity you model, the integrity you walk in, and the inner strength you pass down. And if you want to lead others well, you must first know who you are in Christ. Because before you are a coach, you are a child of God.

### *The Identity Crisis of Today's Coaches*

We live in a world that confuses identity with performance. Social media highlights, headlines, and human praise have many coaches chasing validation over vision. I know because I've been there. There were seasons when I thought my value was in how well my team performed — if we were winning, I was worthy.

If we lost, I felt like a failure. That mindset nearly destroyed my peace and pulled me into pride, anxiety, and ego. Then I realized: performance is not identity. Identity is who you are when no one's clapping. It's who you are when the lights go off, the players go home, and the only eyes on you are the Lord's. "Put on your new nature, created to be like God—truly righteous and holy." — Ephesians 4:24 (NLT)

### How the Seven Deadly Sins Exposed Me

In that season of misalignment, I saw all seven of the enemy's tools show up in my life.

Pride — I took credit for team success instead of glorifying God.

Lust — I battled temptations that tried to creep in through compliments and admiration.

Greed — I made decisions based on personal gain, not team growth.

Gluttony — I wanted to run up the score to feed my ego.

Envy — I compared my program to others instead of celebrating their success.

Wrath — I lashed out in anger when things didn't go my way.

Sloth — I ignored my spiritual growth while overworking my flesh.

And all of that happened because I had forgotten who I was.

### The Power of a Praying Coach

What changed me wasn't just reading more leadership books or going to more clinics — it was prayer. Daily, private, sometimes tear-filled prayer. That's when I discovered the truth: If your identity isn't rooted in Christ, it will be uprooted by crisis. And coaches — we face crisis all the time. Unrealistic expectations. Job insecurity. Judgment from parents. Division among staff. Discouragement from outcomes. Without prayer, those pressures will shape you. With prayer, God will shape you.

### Integrity Is Doing Right When It's Hard

Integrity is more than honesty — it's consistency in righteousness: It's being the same person in the locker room and in the living room. It's speaking truth even when it costs you something. It's treating the bench player with the same respect as the star. "People with integrity walk safely, but those who follow crooked paths will be exposed." — Proverbs 10:9 (NLT) Your players may forget your speech. But they will never forget your consistency. Because your integrity becomes their inspiration. And integrity doesn't come naturally — it's a fruit of being rooted in the Spirit.

### Inner Strength Is More Than Grit

We often celebrate toughness and grind in sports — and that's good. But the most powerful strength isn't found in the weight room or on the practice field. It's found in the Spirit of God within you. "I pray that from his glorious, unlimited resources he will empower you with inner strength through his Spirit." — Ephesians 3:16 (NLT) Inner strength is what keeps you calm when the chaos comes. It's what lets you lead with peace when the pressure is high. It's the Spirit reminding you that God is in control — not the scoreboard.

### Scientific Support for Spiritual Identity

Modern psychology agrees with the Word. Research from the American Psychological Association shows that: Leaders who operate from a secure identity are more resilient under pressure. Emotional regulation (linked to inner strength) is a top predictor of success and influence. Integrity-based leadership is directly correlated with team trust and long-term program health. Translation? What the Bible teaches, science now confirms.

### Real-Life Coaching Moments That Required Prayer

I've been in meetings where I had to stand for righteousness when others wanted to cut corners. I've had moments when I saw a player struggling in silence and the Holy Spirit nudged me to pray, not talk, pray. One time, I sensed a player was on the verge of something dark. I didn't know what, but I felt it. During our stretch period, I laid my hand on his shoulder and whispered a quiet prayer. He looked at me with tears in his eyes and said, "Coach, I needed that." Prayer is discernment. Prayer is covering. Prayer is listening when words don't work.

### You Can't Lead Right If You're Spiritually Off

When I led disconnected from God, I burned out faster. When I led from prayer, I had more patience, more peace, and more purpose. When you lead from your ego, the pressure builds. When you lead from your identity in Christ, the pressure lifts. And the only way to consistently lead from that place is to build your day on prayer.

### Daily Identity Prayer

Wake up and say: "I am not what I do. I am who God says I am."

Before practice: "Lord, lead me today — not my ego."

After conflict: "Lord, align my response with Your truth, not my feelings."

At night: "Thank You, God, for the privilege to lead. Help me grow in integrity and strength."

### Prayer for Identity, Integrity, and Strength

Father, I surrender the false versions of myself — the prideful one, the insecure one, the distracted one. I receive Your truth: that I am Yours. Cleanse me of every sin that tries to distort my purpose. Build my integrity. Strengthen me with Your Spirit. And let my coaching reflect Your presence in every word and action. In Yahshua's (Jesus') name, Amen.

### Reflection & Challenge

Where have I allowed pressure to shape my identity?

Which of the seven deadly sins do I need to actively resist through prayer?

Am I leading from a place of identity or insecurity?

**Challenge:**

For the next 7 days, start each morning with this declaration:

"My identity is in Christ. My strength is from the Spirit. My leadership reflects the Light."

Then write one prayer sentence in your journal each day for yourself as a coach.

# 3

# Chapter 3: Praying for Wisdom Under Pressure

***Because Emotion Without Alignment Can Wreck Leadership***

There is no classroom quite like the sidelines. No pulpit quite like the locker room. And no pressure like the kind coaches face when decisions must be made in real time — while the crowd yells, the clock ticks, and the outcome weighs heavily. Pressure is part of the job. But wisdom? Wisdom is the weapon. And the only way to receive wisdom under pressure is through prayer.

***Pressure Doesn't Create You — It Reveals You***

Early in my coaching career, I believed pressure proved I was strong. I thrived on it. Called audibles. Barked orders. Pushed through. But over time, I realized something deeper: Pressure doesn't develop your character. It exposes what's already there. When I wasn't spiritually grounded, I made emotional decisions. I snapped in team meetings. I blamed players too quickly. I felt like I had to control everything. And that led to overthinking, stress, and spiritual exhaustion. Then I found this truth: "If you need wisdom, ask our generous God, and he will give it to you. He will not rebuke you for asking." — *James 1:5 (NLT)* I started asking. Before games. Before tough conversations. Before meetings with administration. Before responding to disrespect. I didn't just prepare the playbook — I prepared my heart.

### The Real Enemies: Fear, Anger, and Ego

Let's be honest — pressure isn't just about making the right call. It's about how we handle fear, anger, and ego when we're under fire. **Fear** of failure or letting people down. **Anger** when things don't go as planned. **Ego** when we think we're the only ones who can fix it. But wisdom from God cuts through all of that. Proverbs 3:5–6 (NLT) says: "Trust in the Lord with all your heart; do not depend on your own understanding. Seek his will in all you do, and he will show you which path to take." I've seen coaches self-destruct not because of their knowledge, but because of their lack of inner peace. Emotional reactions sabotage good intentions. That's why wisdom is more valuable than talent. It's what turns chaos into clarity. Emotion into leadership.

### The Science of Wise Decision-Making

Neuroscience confirms what scripture says. Under high stress, the amygdala in your brain hijacks rational thinking. Coaches who train themselves to pause, breathe, and pray activate the prefrontal cortex — the part of the brain responsible for decision-making, empathy, and problem-solving. That means your prayer life literally rewires your brain to respond, not react.

So when a coach says, "I don't have time to pray — I've got too much going on," I say, "You can't afford not to pray."

### How Yahshua (Jesus) Led Under Pressure

There is no better model than Yahshua (Jesus). He faced criticism, betrayal, and impossible decisions. And how did He respond? He withdrew to pray (Luke 5:16). He listened to the Father before speaking. He chose silence over reaction (Matthew 27:12–14). He washed feet instead of proving status (John 13:5). Yahshua (Jesus) never panicked — not because He wasn't human, but because He was anchored. We, as coaches, are called to the same: To lead from the Spirit, not from stress.

### My Moment of Weakness Became a Moment of Wisdom

There was a time I was in a must-win situation. The pressure was on — media was there, scouts were watching. I was coaching with fire... but inside, I was unraveling. One of my players made a mistake that cost us a key possession. In my flesh, I wanted to pull him, yell, and make an example. But instead, I paused. I prayed — quietly. And I felt the Holy Spirit say: "Speak life, not frustration." So I looked that young man in the eyes and said, "Shake it off. I believe in you." He ended up making the game-winning play two drives later. That day, I didn't just win a game — I won a heart.

### Practical Ways to Stay Spiritually Sharp Under Pressure

1. Breathe before you speak – Even one deep breath while praying, "God guide me," can change everything.

2. Establish pre-game and post-game prayer habits – Let prayer bookend your leadership.
3. Create a short list of scriptures – Have go-to verses in your mind to repeat when under stress.
4. Develop a "pressure team" – Identify 2–3 people who will pray for you consistently in your leadership.
5. Memorize James 1:5 – Make wisdom your first ask, not your last resort.

### Prayer for Wisdom Under Pressure

*Lord, I surrender my emotions to You. Help me respond, not react. Give me wisdom that is pure, peace-loving, and full of mercy. Quiet my mind so I can hear Your voice when the noise is loud. Make me the kind of coach who leads with grace and discernment — in wins, losses, and all the moments in between. In Yahshua's (Jesus') name, Amen.*

### Reflection & Challenge

What emotion tends to lead my decisions when I'm under pressure?

Where have I seen the difference between reacting and responding?

Do I invite God into my decision-making — or do I wait until after things go wrong?

**Challenge:**
This week, identify one high-pressure moment (game, meet-

ing, or tough convo).

Pause before it begins. Take 30 seconds and pray.

Ask for wisdom. Then act.

Write down what happened and how you felt afterward.

4

# Chapter 4: Praying for Your Players

***Speaking Life, Purpose, and Protection into the Next Generation***

Every coach will leave a mark — but not every coach will leave a legacy. That legacy doesn't come from your win/loss record. It doesn't come from how many players went D1. It comes from how you made your players feel — and more importantly, how you led them spiritually. When you pray for your players — when you speak life over them, call out purpose within them, and cover them in protection — you're not just coaching a team. You're building men and women of God.

***They're Not Just Athletes. They're Sons and Daughters of God.***

Early in my coaching career, I viewed players through the lens of performance. Who could produce? Who was tough enough? Who had potential? But over time, God softened my heart. He reminded me that these young men and women are more than bodies on a field or names on a depth chart. They are His children. "Children are a gift from the Lord; they are a reward from him."

— Psalm 127:3 (NLT) That means every player is a soul. Every soul has a story. And every story matters to God.

### The Weight They Carry, the Battles We Can't See

Some of your players smile in public but cry in silence. Some come from chaos — addiction, abuse, broken homes. Others are silently battling identity confusion, depression, or insecurity. And they may never tell you with words. But they will show you with their behavior. I've had players act out, not because they were disrespectful — but because they were drowning. I've coached athletes with incredible potential who struggled with anxiety so paralyzing they couldn't perform under pressure. I've seen kids lash out in anger who were really asking, "Do I matter?" And what they need isn't just correction. They need covering.

### Intercession Is the Coach's Secret Weapon

To intercede means to stand in the gap. When you pray for your players, you're not just saying words — you're positioning yourself between them and the forces trying to take them out. "I urge you, first of all, to pray for all people. Ask God to help them; intercede on their behalf, and give thanks for them." — 1 Timothy 2:1 (NLT) You don't always need to confront a player. Sometimes, you need to confront the spirit behind what they're going through — in prayer. I've seen players transform without a single lecture. I simply started praying for them. Quietly. By name. And over time, their demeanor, work ethic, and attitude shifted. Because prayer softens what pride defends.

### Speaking Life Over Performance

Too many coaches only speak when things go wrong. But players don't just need correction — they need confirmation. They need someone who says: "I see greatness in you." "You matter more than what you produce." "You were created on purpose, for a purpose." "The tongue can bring death or life; those who love to talk will reap the consequences." — Proverbs 18:21 (NLT) When we speak life, we unlock potential. When we pray life, we break spiritual strongholds. I challenge you: Before every practice or film session, say one life-giving sentence to each player. It may be awkward at first, but it will become normal — and transformational.

### Science Proves What the Bible Already Taught

Research from the University of Southern California shows that: Students with at least one adult who speaks consistent affirmation over them show higher academic and emotional resilience. Coaches ranked just behind parents as the most influential voice in teen development. And athletes who experience consistent verbal support are 3x more likely to persist through failure and develop leadership skills. Translation? You don't need to preach. You need to be present and prayerful.

### Stories from the Sideline: Covering in the Spirit

I had a player who came to every practice, never complained, always worked hard — but something seemed off. He was withdrawn. Unfocused. He wasn't responding to my typical encouragement. So I started praying for him every morning.

No lectures. Just covering. Weeks later, he opened up. He was dealing with severe family trauma at home. He said, "Coach, I felt like someone was praying for me — I don't know why, but it got lighter." That's the power of intercession.

### Who Else Needs Prayer? Everyone.

Don't stop at players. Pray for: Their families — for peace, healing, and restoration. Their future — college, relationships, and purpose. Their health — protection from injury and mental burnout. Their hearts — healing from unseen wounds. Their walk with God — even if they don't yet know Him. "I have no greater joy than to hear that my children are walking in the truth." — 3 John 1:4 (NLT)

### Spoken Prayer for Players

Father, thank You for every player You've entrusted to me. I cover them with Your love and protection. Speak to them in their dreams, quiet their fears, and awaken their purpose. Let them know they are more than what they do — they are who You say they are. Use me to speak life. Help me love them even when they push back. Guide me in truth and grace. In Yahshua's (Jesus') name, Amen.

### Reflection & Challenge

Who on your team do you sense is silently struggling?

Do your players feel covered by your leadership or judged by it?

Have you made prayer for your team a habit or a reaction?

***Challenge:***

This week, write down the names of your players.

Next to each name, write one word you want to speak over them: "Leader," "Peace," "Purpose," "Healing."

Then, pray that word over them privately — and speak it to them publicly when the moment is right.

5

# Chapter 5: Praying for Team Unity and Chemistry

**Building a Bond That Wins Without the Scoreboard**

You can have five-star talent and a championship playbook — but without unity, it will crumble. You can have average athletes with a shared purpose — and they will shock the world. Unity isn't about skill. It's about spirit. And as coaches, we are not just developing players — we are cultivating connection. Connection to each other. Connection to purpose. Connection to Christ.

**Unity Is the Superpower Most Coaches Overlook**

In my 10+ years of coaching, I've seen this over and over: I've coached great players on divided teams — and they underperformed. I've coached average athletes with tight bonds — and they overachieved. The difference wasn't the playbook. The difference was prayer, trust, and connection. Unity turns a group of individuals into a team. Chemistry turns effort into execution. And both are built through intentional leadership and spiritual covering.

### Disunity Doesn't Just Happen — It's Cultivated in Silence

Teams don't fall apart overnight. Disunity creeps in when: Players gossip instead of speaking truth. Coaches form cliques instead of one voice. Accountability disappears and ego takes over. The enemy loves division, and he works subtly. "A house divided against itself will not stand." — Matthew 12:25 (NLT) Division among your staff, between your players, or between leadership and team — it weakens your authority. It creates confusion, mistrust, and ultimately failure in the areas that matter most.

### Spiritual Unity Begins With You

As the head goes, so goes the body. If the leader isn't spiritually aligned, the team won't be either. You must: Pray for unity consistently. Speak peace over every meeting and practice. Discern division when it's hiding behind sarcasm or silence. Rebuke ego — even your own — when it threatens team cohesion. "Always be humble and gentle. Be patient with each other, making allowance for each other's faults because of your love. Make every effort to keep yourselves united in the Spirit." — Ephesians 4:2–3 (NLT) Unity isn't perfection. Unity is choosing grace. It's communication over confusion. It's one vision over many egos.

### Chemistry Is Built in the Invisible Moments

It's not just about time spent together — it's about the tone set. Are your captains speaking life or tearing others down? Are your veterans modeling humility or entitlement? Are your team rituals and pregame habits rooted in alignment or chaos? Chemistry starts with culture. And culture starts with spirit.

### Prayer Is the Glue That Fuses Spirit and Skill

When you pray over your team daily, by name, and with purpose, something changes. Not immediately, but consistently. I've had seasons where I sensed invisible tension among players. Instead of lecturing, I started covering. I'd walk the locker room before players arrived and quietly pray over the chairs. "Lord, remove division." "Let brotherhood be restored." "Let love win over pride." By the end of the season, those same players who wouldn't look each other in the eye were laughing, serving, and winning — not just games, but each other's trust. That's the power of praying unity into existence.

### Science Confirms the Power of Belonging

Studies from the Journal of Sport & Exercise Psychology show: Teams with higher social cohesion perform better under pressure. Players who feel emotionally connected to their team are 60% more resilient after losses. Trust and communication reduce anxiety, improve focus, and increase collective performance. And you know what builds those qualities? Intentional, spiritually grounded leadership.

### Create a Unity Rhythm in Your Program

1. Weekly Team Prayer Huddles — not just before games, but

before workouts or film.

2. Player-Led Gratitude Circles — give space for your athletes to honor one another.

3. Conflict Resolution Through Prayer — when tension rises, bring players together and pray first, speak second.

4. Unity Verses of the Week — simple NLT scriptures printed and posted.

Unity isn't one big speech. It's a thousand small reinforcements.

### When You Lead From the Spirit, You Lead With Clarity

The most unified teams I've coached weren't the most talented — but they were the most aligned. They were accountable. Vulnerable. Faithful. They were a reflection of the leadership we modeled. "Live in harmony with each other. Let there be no divisions... Rather, be of one mind, united in thought and purpose."
    — 1 Corinthians 1:10 (NLT)

### Prayer for Team Unity and Chemistry

Father, I thank You for this team You've entrusted to me. Let Your Spirit of unity fill every conversation, every drill, and every moment. Remove comparison, jealousy, and ego. Let us be of one heart, one mind, and one mission — to reflect Your love. Heal every rift. Mend every broken bond. And let the love between teammates be louder than any scoreboard. In Yahshua's (Jesus') name, Amen.

### Reflection & Challenge

Where have I noticed signs of division or disunity?

Am I modeling spiritual and emotional unity to my players?

Have I been praying intentionally over my team's chemistry — or just their performance?

### Challenge:

Choose one practice this week to dedicate entirely to team bonding and spiritual unity.

No X's and O's. No wins and losses. Just intentional prayer, sharing, laughter, and love.

Then write down what you observed — and continue building from there.

# 6

# Chapter 9: Praying for Your Career and Calling

## *Trusting God's Plan Through Doors Opened and Closed*

Your calling isn't your title. Your purpose isn't your position. And your value doesn't come from a win percentage. As coaches, we often wrap our identity in our career — promotions, job offers, accolades. But the truth is, God cares more about who you're becoming than where you're coaching. Your career is a platform. Your calling is a kingdom assignment.

## *Coaching Was Always More Than a Job*

I knew from a young age that I was called to reach the next generation. I loved sports. I loved strategy. I loved competition. But more than anything, I loved seeing growth in young people — not just in strength or skill, but in confidence and character. For a long time, I thought I was just a "coach." But I now understand — I was always a minister in disguise. "For we are God's masterpiece. He has created us anew in Christ Yahshua's

(Jesus), so we can do the good things he planned for us long ago." — Ephesians 2:10 (NLT)

### When the Path Doesn't Make Sense

There was a season when everything seemed to fall apart. A job opportunity I was sure was from God fell through. I faced criticism. I questioned if I was good enough. I even questioned if I should keep coaching. But in the silence, the Lord reminded me: "You're not here because of approval. You're here because of obedience." And obedience doesn't always look like elevation — sometimes it looks like refinement. "We can make our plans, but the Lord determines our steps." — Proverbs 16:9 (NLT) God is not just concerned with your next job — He's concerned with your next level of faith.

### The Idolization of Career in Coaching Culture

Let's be honest — in the coaching world, your worth is often judged by: What level you coach at. How many championships you've won. Who you've trained that "made it". And while those things can be blessings, they can also become idols. Your calling is not to climb — it's to follow Christ. If He promotes you — praise Him. If He pauses you — trust Him. If He redirects you — surrender.

### What to Do When Doors Close

Closed doors don't mean you're not called. They often mean you're being protected or prepared. I've been turned down for jobs I was sure I was ready for — only to look back and realize I wasn't ready spiritually. If you've been overlooked, misunderstood, or feel "stuck" in your role — know this: You are not forgotten. You are being forged. "Don't grow weary in doing good, for at just the right time, you will reap a harvest if you don't give up." — Galatians 6:9 (NLT)

### Calling Is Bigger Than a Contract

Some of the most anointed coaches I've ever met don't coach in big arenas. They coach in: Inner-city gyms, small schools with no budget, volunteer youth leagues, and community outreach programs but their impact is eternal. They may not be making headlines — but they're making disciples.

### Discerning Between Ambition and Assignment

Here's a test I've used in prayer: Am I chasing this opportunity for applause — or alignment? Will this open door stretch my faith — or feed my ego? Am I willing to stay if God asks me to be faithful in the "small" place? "Seek the Kingdom of God above all else, and live righteously, and he will give you everything you need." — Matthew 6:33 (NLT) If you seek His Kingdom first — He'll open the right doors at the right time.

### When You Feel Invisible

You might feel like your career is stuck in neutral. You're not moving backward — but you're not moving forward either. That's when the enemy whispers: "You're being passed over." "You're wasting time." "You're falling behind." But God says: "Be still and know that I am God." — Psalm 46:10 (NLT) Stillness isn't weakness — it's preparation.

### Coaching at God's Speed

Just like in The Method Man, where we talked about "God's speed" — spiritual alignment often moves differently than worldly hustle. Let your faith set the pace, not frustration. God is more committed to your development than your destination.

### Prayer for Your Career and Calling

Lord, thank You for calling me into coaching. Help me not to idolize the next job or fear the next step. Teach me to follow, not just lead. Whether You open a door or close it, let me trust Your hand. Let me walk with humility, serve with joy, and stay anchored in Your purpose. My career belongs to You. Use it for Your glory. In Yahshua's (Jesus') name, Amen.

### Reflection & Challenge

Am I pursuing positions or staying rooted in purpose?

Where have I allowed fear or frustration to cloud my trust in God's plan?

Have I stopped praying about my career — or only prayed when things got hard?

### Challenge:

Spend 15 minutes this week journaling your "coaching testimony."

Reflect on how God brought you here.

Then, write a prayer declaring that your future is in His hands — not yours.

# Chapter 6: Praying Through Wins and Losses

### *Embracing God's Purpose in Every Outcome*

In sports, we're trained to chase victory and avoid defeat. But in the Kingdom of God, every outcome carries purpose. Wins may build confidence — but losses build character. Wins may get attention — but losses get your attention. As coaches, it's easy to ride the emotional roller coaster of the season — up when we win, discouraged when we lose. But God's purpose isn't tied to your record. It's tied to your response.

### *The True Scoreboard Is Spiritual*

I used to measure success by wins, trophies, and titles. I thought I was doing my job if my team performed. But deep down, I knew something was off. I was coaching from performance, not from purpose. That's when the Lord revealed something powerful: "People judge by outward appearance, but the Lord looks at the heart." — 1 Samuel 16:7 (NLT) God isn't checking your win column. He's checking your heart column. Because wins don't define legacy. Obedience does.

### Losses Hurt, But They Also Heal

I'll never forget a heartbreaking playoff loss that left our entire program stunned. We were favored to win. We were loaded with talent. We had every reason to believe we'd go all the way. But one mistake. One moment. One shift — and it was over. I was angry. Not at my players — at myself, at God, at the moment. But after the locker room emptied and the noise faded, I sat alone and prayed. And God spoke: "This loss isn't punishment. It's positioning." That loss birthed hunger in our team. Humility. Unity. We came back stronger, wiser, and more surrendered. "God blesses those who mourn, for they will be comforted." — Matthew 5:4 (NLT)

### Wins Must Be Stewarded Too

We talk about stewardship after loss — but do we steward victory with humility? A win can either fill you with pride or fuel you with praise. A winning streak can make you bold — or make you blind. I've seen teams win big and lose their identity. I've seen coaches win games and lose their families. Every win must be prayed over. "Lord, help me stay humble. Help me remember this is Yours." "Pride leads to disgrace, but with humility comes wisdom." — Proverbs 11:2 (NLT) Celebrate — yes. But don't crown yourself king after one win. God is still the Coach. You're just the vessel.

### When the Scoreboard Lies

33

There are games where you lose — but your players grow, and your culture deepens. There are games where you win — but your ego grows, and your character weakens. So ask yourself: Did we honor each other today? Did we grow in grace today? Did I reflect Christ today? If yes — you won, no matter the score. "Let your roots grow down into him... Then your faith will grow strong in the truth you were taught." — Colossians 2:7 (NLT)

### Pray Through It All

Win or lose — pray. Before the buzzer sounds, center your heart. After the final whistle, thank Him — no matter the result. In every team meeting, remind them: who we are is greater than what we did. Players will forget the final score. But they won't forget your consistency.

### When Players Are Broken After a Loss

This is one of the hardest moments in coaching — when you see a senior crying, a leader blaming themselves, a team devastated. Here's what I've learned: Don't fix. Sit with them. Don't rush. Let them process. Don't preach. Pray. "The Lord is close to the brokenhearted; he rescues those whose spirits are crushed." — Psalm 34:18 (NLT) I've knelt next to players who could barely breathe through tears and simply prayed: "God, show them this pain has purpose. Wrap them in peace. Redeem what feels broken." That moment became more powerful than any win.

### Don't Coach From the Highs and Lows

If your emotions rise and fall with every result, you'll lead inconsistently. But if your foundation is prayer, you'll lead with peace, even in chaos. That's what players need. Not perfection. Not a flawless game plan. They need a coach who is anchored in purpose.

### Prayer for Wins and Losses

Lord, thank You for every victory — and every lesson hidden in defeat. Teach me to lead with grace, no matter the outcome. Keep me humble in the high moments and anchored in the hard ones. Let my players see that I trust You, win or lose. Use every result to refine us. Let this season be about Your glory, not mine. In Yahshua's (Jesus') name, Amen.

### Reflection & Challenge

How do I personally respond to wins? Do I reflect or relax?

How do I process losses? Do I hide, blame, or invite God in?

Do my players know that prayer is our foundation — not just tradition?

Challenge:
   Create a post-game prayer ritual.
   Whether in a huddle or privately, begin to end every competition with a prayer of surrender.
   Wins, losses, injuries, or comebacks — give it all back to God.

# Chapter 7: Praying for Parents and Families

*Partnering with the Home to Raise Whole-Hearted Champions*

You coach more than players — You coach their pain. You coach their personality. You coach their backgrounds, their burdens, and their belief systems. And behind every player is a home — sometimes whole, sometimes broken. Sometimes supportive, sometimes silent. But always significant. As coaches, we often focus only on what we can see: speed, skill, strength. But the greatest impact you'll ever have may come from how you pray for what you cannot see.

### Behind Every Jersey Is a Story

I've coached players with incredible athleticism but emotional walls built from trauma. I've seen kids crumble under pressure — not because they're weak, but because they're carrying the weight of what's happening at home. Some have loving parents. Some have absent ones. Some go home to chaos, hunger, abuse, or silence. You don't always know the backstory. But God does. "The Lord hears his people when they call to him for help. He rescues them from all their troubles." — Psalm 34:17 (NLT) That's why prayer isn't just for the athlete. It's for the household.

### When the Home Is Hurting, the Player Suffers Silently

I've seen players show up with their heads down and hearts heavy. They wouldn't say much — but their body language preached pain. One player in particular was battling depression. His father was verbally abusive, and his mother was trying to hold the family together. Every time he missed a play, it wasn't just frustration — it was fear of being a disappointment. I began praying for him — but also for his home. Not just "Lord, help him perform," but, "Lord, heal what's happening behind closed doors." Over time, I saw joy return to his game. He started trusting again. Not just me — but himself.

### Coaches Are Spiritual Guardians, Not Just Game Planners

You may never sit at the family dinner table, but your voice carries into that house. How you speak to your players. How you affirm them. How you correct them. It echoes beyond the field. So ask yourself: Am I praying for the healing of their household? Am I covering their parents, even if I don't always agree with them? Am I lifting their home in the Spirit, even when I only see a sliver of it? "Share each other's burdens, and in this way obey the law of Christ." — Galatians 6:2 (NLT)

### Families Are Often Fighting Invisible Battles

Divorce in progress

Financial hardship

Addiction

Mental health struggles

Grief from loss

Cultural clashes

Absent fathers

Overbearing expectations

You don't always know — but God does. And your intercession could be the reason healing begins in that home.

### Practical Ways to Pray for Families

1. By Name — Write a list of players' families and pray intentionally.

2. By Need — If you know they're facing something specific, lift it.

3. By Spirit — Ask the Holy Spirit to intercede even when you don't know the details.

"And the Holy Spirit helps us in our weakness... the Holy Spirit

prays for us with groanings that cannot be expressed in words."
— Romans 8:26 (NLT)

### You May Be the Only Covering That Family Has

Some players don't attend church. Some families have never been prayed for — ever. When you pray, you open a window of grace into that household. Whether you're coaching public school, private, or community programs — your spiritual role goes far beyond the sidelines.

### Bless the Parents — Even When It's Difficult

Let's be real — not every parent is easy to deal with. Some criticize. Some overstep. Some disrespect your boundaries. But don't let offense rob you of obedience. Pray for them anyway. Bless those who misunderstand you. Honor those who show up and those who never do. "But I say, love your enemies! Pray for those who persecute you!" — Matthew 5:44 (NLT) The same grace you give your players — extend it to the ones who raised them.

### Stories That Prove It Matters

I once had a player whose mom was battling cancer. He never told anyone. He showed up, worked hard, but carried a sadness he couldn't explain. When I found out, I started praying for her healing — and for his heart. Months later, his mother pulled me aside and said, "I don't know what you're doing, but he comes home lighter. Happier. I think God's working through you." That wasn't my doing. That was prayer doing what words couldn't.

### Prayer for Parents and Families

Lord, thank You for every family represented on my team. I pray for peace in their homes, strength for the parents, provision for their needs, and healing where there's hurt. Even if I never step into their living room, let Your Spirit enter in. Use me as a bridge — not just for players, but for households. Let revival start at home, even through this team. In Yahshua's (Jesus') name, Amen.

### Reflection & Challenge

Which families have I unintentionally overlooked in my prayers?

Have I allowed offense or judgment to block me from praying over parents who frustrate me?

Am I spiritually covering the full ecosystem my players come from — or just the athlete in front of me?

### Challenge:

This week, write a family blessing. Print it, email it, or pray it silently.

Something like: "May your home be filled with peace. May your family be strengthened. And may God's presence be felt in every conversation, every struggle, and every breakthrough."

Then watch what happens — in their homes... and in your heart.

# Chapter 8: Praying for Your Coaching Staff and Leadership

*Maintaining Humility, Vision, and Alignment in the Trenches*

The enemy's most effective tactic in any organization — from a church to a team — is division among leadership. If he can disrupt the unity at the top, the mission collapses at the bottom. That's why the strength of your program doesn't begin with your players — It begins with your coaching staff. Whether you have 3 assistants or 13, unity, humility, and spiritual alignment must be guarded like a championship trophy.

### The Staff Is the Spine of the Program

A healthy spine supports the body. A fractured spine disables movement. I've served on coaching staffs where unity was real — shared mission, shared mindset, shared heart. And I've also been on staffs where pride crept in, egos clashed, and behind-the-scenes cliques poisoned the culture. Disunity in leadership always bleeds into the team. "A house divided against itself will not stand." — Mark 3:25 (NLT) You don't need more talent — You need more unity.

### The Clique of Christ, Not Competition

One of the most dangerous dynamics I've seen is coaches forming "sides." A few assistants side with one coach, another group with someone else, and passive-aggression fills the air. What should be one voice becomes many whispers. And the locker room starts to echo that tension. Here's what I've learned: No one wins when coaches compete for attention or control. A divided staff cannot build a unified team. There should be one clique — the clique of Christ. That means: One vision. One culture. One Spirit. "Make every effort to keep yourselves united in the Spirit, binding yourselves together with peace." — Ephesians 4:3 (NLT)

### Check the Ego at the Door — Daily

As leaders, pride can creep in subtly. You want credit for a new scheme. You feel overlooked in a staff meeting. You're frustrated you didn't get promoted. But pride is a silent killer of culture. "Pride goes before destruction, and haughtiness before a fall." — Proverbs 16:18 (NLT) I now begin every staff meeting with one prayer: "Lord, remove pride. Align us with Your purpose. Make us one." When ego is removed, purpose takes its place.

### Cover Your Staff Like Family

These aren't just co-workers. They're your spiritual teammates in the most important mission — shaping souls. So ask yourself: Have I prayed for my assistants this week? Have I checked in on their personal life? Have I encouraged them — or just evaluated them? Some of your assistants may be dealing with depression. Some may feel invisible. Some are battling things at home you can't see. Cover them in prayer. Speak life into them. And never assume they're okay just because they show up.

### How to Cultivate a Spirit-Led Staff Culture

1. Start Staff Meetings in Prayer — even 2 minutes can shift the tone.

2. Rotate a Weekly Staff Devotion or Scripture — give each coach a voice.

3. Encourage Open Dialogue — spiritually and emotionally.

4. Affirm Each Coach Publicly — highlight what they bring to the team.

5. Fast Together Once a Season — for team unity, safety, and purpose.

When coaches pray together — they lead together. When coaches war in the Spirit together — they win in culture and character.

### Science Supports Spirit-Led Leadership

A study from the Center for Creative Leadership showed: Teams led by emotionally intelligent, humble leaders perform higher under pressure. Spiritual wellness in leadership correlates with better conflict resolution and decision-making. Staff cohesion directly influences player morale and team success. Translation? What the Spirit teaches, the data now confirms.

### Your Staff Reflects You

You are the head. They are the arms and legs. If your spirit is off, the body feels it. But if you model humility, honor, and prayer — they will follow. Even your unspoken behaviors become the staff standard. So don't just expect unity. Create it. Model it. Pray it.

### Prayer for Coaching Staff and Leadership

Lord, thank You for every coach You've placed on this staff. Remove ego, offense, pride, and division from our midst. Give us one heart, one mind, and one voice. Let us encourage each other, support each other, and be led by Your Spirit above all. Let this coaching staff be a light to our team, our school, and our community. In Yahshua's (Jesus') name, Amen.

### Reflection & Challenge

Is there any tension or misalignment I've been avoiding addressing?

Have I actively prayed for my coaching staff, or just worked alongside them?

Am I leading my staff with humility or from hierarchy?

**Challenge:**

Send an encouraging text to every member of your staff this week.

Pray for them by name. Speak one sentence of life into who they are and what they bring.

Then, start your next meeting with prayer — and watch the culture shift.

# 10

# Chapter 10: Praying for Your School and Community

### Becoming a Lighthouse Beyond the Scoreboard

You are not just the coach of a team. You are the spiritual thermostat of a school. You are the lighthouse in a community where storms are raging. Your job description may say "coach," but your calling is bigger than wins and rosters. You are a presence carrier, and the light you carry doesn't stop at the gym or field. It extends into hallways, households, and hearts.

### The Coach Everyone Watches

Whether you realize it or not: Teachers notice how you speak to your players. Administrators see how you lead under pressure. Custodians and security guards feel the energy you bring into spaces. Students — even ones you don't coach — are watching who you are. You are influencing more than your team. You're influencing a culture. "You are the light of the world—like a city on a hilltop that cannot be hidden." — Matthew 5:14 (NLT)

46

### The Atmosphere You Carry Can Shift the Whole Building

I've walked into schools where the energy was heavy — fights in the hallways, low morale among staff, and discouragement in the air. But I've also seen what happens when one Spirit-filled coach enters with intention: Peace rises. Respect increases. Students feel safe. Staff feel seen. God's presence becomes palpable. You don't have to say "Yahshua (Jesus)" to shine Yahshua (Jesus). Your posture, your patience, your prayers — they preach louder than any words.

### Start With Silent Prayer

I began a habit years ago of walking my school silently before the day started. I'd walk through the gym, around the lockers, past classrooms — and I'd pray under my breath: "Lord, protect this hallway." "God, touch the heart of that student." "Let Your Spirit flood this space." And over time, I watched God move: Fights reduced. Conversations deepened. Students came to me asking for prayer, unprompted. The building felt different. Not because I was loud, but because I was prayerful.

### When You Pray for the Community, You Raise the Standard

Our communities are filled with: Fatherlessness, Violence, Poverty, Addiction, Depression, Disconnection. We can't fix all of that alone, but we can intercede. We can show up to town halls. We can partner with local leaders. We can pray over city blocks, schools, parks, and neighborhoods. "Work for the peace and prosperity of the city where I sent you... Pray to the Lord for it, for its welfare will determine your welfare." — Jeremiah 29:7

(NLT) When you pray over your city, you're planting seeds of revival.

### Small Acts, Big Impact

Greet every student, not just athletes. Learn the names of custodians, cafeteria workers, and front desk staff. Show up for the drama department or band concert, not just sports events. Invite others into prayer — quietly, respectfully, but intentionally. Presence builds trust. Prayer builds transformation.

### When Tragedy Hits, Be the Rock

I've seen schools rocked by student deaths, family tragedies, and community violence. And in those moments, the team looks to the coach. So does the school. So does the neighborhood. That's why you must be spiritually prepared before the storm hits. Your peace under pressure becomes someone else's anchor. "The Lord is close to the brokenhearted; he rescues those whose spirits are crushed." — Psalm 34:18 (NLT)

### Invite God Into the Entire Campus

This isn't just your team. This is your mission field. Pray over: Your principal — for wisdom and vision. Your teachers — for encouragement and strength. Your office staff — for peace in their interactions. Your school counselors — for discernment and compassion. The opposing team and coaches — for safety and brotherhood.

### When the Community Knows You're Praying

It changes how they see coaching. Parents begin to respect your leadership differently. Students outside your program feel your presence. Local leaders start coming to you for wisdom. Revival becomes relational, not just religious. This is how we become lighthouses — not with a spotlight, but with consistent spiritual illumination.

### Prayer for School and Community

Lord, thank You for placing me here — in this school, in this neighborhood, with these people. Let me carry Your light boldly, even without saying a word. Use me to uplift the discouraged, cover the unseen, and pray for every space I enter. I speak peace over every hallway, hope over every classroom, and unity over our community. Let Your Spirit move through me — and let revival begin with love. In Yahshua's (Jesus') name, Amen.

### Reflection & Challenge

Have I been intentionally praying over the full school environment — or only my team?

Do I show up in ways that uplift the community and support the full body of students and staff?

Is my spiritual leadership visible through humility, kindness, and presence — or hidden behind performance?

### Challenge:
Take a prayer walk around your campus.
Pray silently as you pass by different areas.

49

Then, ask God to show you one non-athlete student or staff member you can affirm or encourage this week — and do it.

# 11

# Chapter 11: Praying Against Burnout and Spiritual Warfare

### Resting, Resetting, and Protecting Your Peace

Behind every passionate coach is a person fighting battles no one sees. And while we teach our players to push through pain, press past fatigue, and "grind harder," the truth is: Many of us are coaching on empty. The smile is there. The passion still flickers. But deep inside? You're tired. Drained. Spiritually depleted. This chapter is your reminder: You are not weak for needing rest. You are wise for protecting your peace.

### Burnout Is Real, and It's Spiritual

Burnout isn't just about being tired — it's what happens when you've poured out more than you've allowed God to pour in. You give, and give, and give. You motivate others while silently falling apart. You pray for your players — but forget to pray for yourself. You correct others — but neglect your own spiritual reset. "Come to me, all of you who are weary and carry heavy burdens, and I will give you rest." — Matthew 11:28 (NLT) Coaches, rest is not laziness. Rest is obedience.

### The Warning Signs

Here are some signs you may be running on empty: Quick to anger, Emotionally numb, Avoiding people or responsibilities, Cynicism or resentment, Sleeplessness or anxiety, Decreased motivation or joy in coaching, These aren't personality traits. These are spiritual red flags. And the solution isn't another podcast, clinic, or motivational video. It's presence — God's presence.

### Yahshua (Jesus) Withdrew. So Should You.

Even Yahshua (Jesus), the Son of God — withdrew from the crowds. "But Yahshua (Jesus) often withdrew to the wilderness for prayer." — Luke 5:16 (NLT) If Yahshua (Jesus) needed solitude to recharge, so do you. Not isolation. Not quitting. But intentional time to be refilled by the Father.

### Spiritual Warfare in Coaching

You're not just leading practices. You're waging war against: Identity confusion, depression or suicide in youth, lust, greed, ego, envy, division, pride among staff, and darkness trying to reach your students through media, trauma, and broken homes. This is warfare. And the only way to win is to be spiritually armed. "Put on all of God's armor so that you will be able to stand firm against all strategies of the devil." — Ephesians 6:11 (NLT)

### The Armor You Need Daily

1. The Helmet of Salvation — Remember who you are and whose you are.

2. The Breastplate of Righteousness — Guard your heart and emotions.

3. The Shield of Faith — Deflect lies, attacks, and discouragement.

4. The Sword of the Spirit — Stay rooted in the Word.

5. The Shoes of Peace — Walk with calm confidence, not anxiety.

6. The Belt of Truth — Stay grounded in what God says — not your feelings.

Don't coach without your armor. Don't lead without being covered.

### When You Don't Feel Like Praying

This is real. There are days when you don't have words. You're not mad at God — just exhausted. That's when Scripture and silence become your sanctuary. "The Holy Spirit helps us in our weakness... the Spirit pleads for us in harmony with God's own will." — Romans 8:26–27 (NLT)

### Building a Lifestyle of Spiritual Reset

1. Sabbath a Day Weekly — Take one day to pause and recharge.

2. Morning Moments — Even 10 minutes with God can set your tone.

3. Digital Detox Weekly — Log off. Be still. Breathe.

4. Speak Life to Yourself — You are not what you do. You are a child of God.

5. Check Your Circle — Surround yourself with people who refill, not drain you.

### *When You Lead While Empty, You Leave the Door Open*

If you're not covered in prayer, you'll coach from the flesh. If you're not rooted in truth, your emotions will lead. And if you don't pause, your burnout will break what you were called to build. Protect your peace. Your purpose depends on it.

### *Prayer Against Burnout and Spiritual Warfare*

Lord, I confess I've been running on empty. I've been pouring out, but I need You to pour in. Restore my soul. Rebuild my mind. Refresh my spirit. Protect me from burnout. Remind me I'm not the Savior — You are. Let me lead from Your strength, not mine. I put on Your armor today. Cover me, God. In Yahshua's (Jesus') name, Amen.

### *Reflection & Challenge*

What signs of burnout have I been ignoring?

Am I giving more to others than I'm receiving from God?

Have I made time with God a non-negotiable — or just an option?

**Challenge:**

This week, take one full evening or morning to unplug. No coaching. No planning.

Just silence, prayer, and rest.

Then write down one word God whispers to you — and carry it into the rest of your season.

# 12

# Chapter 12: The Lifestyle of a Praying Coach

***Daily Habits That Keep You Rooted in Purpose and Prayer***

You've come a long way — through wins and losses, victories and valleys, brokenness and breakthroughs. You've prayed for your players, your staff, your school, and your soul. But the truth is: the work never stops. And that's why prayer must become more than a response — it must become a rhythm. This chapter is not a conclusion — it's a playbook. A spiritual framework to keep you centered and surrendered. Because the praying coach doesn't just pray before big games. He prays as a lifestyle.

***Great Coaches Have Systems.   Great Spiritual Leaders Have Rhythms.***

You don't leave practices or film sessions to chance. You have a plan. But many of us try to grow spiritually without a system — and we wonder why we fall into dryness or distraction. Prayer needs to become your default, not your last resort. And the best way to make that happen is to build it into your daily rhythm. "Never stop praying. Be thankful in all circumstances, for this is God's will for you who belong to Christ Yahshua (Jesus)." — 1 Thessalonians 5:17–18 (NLT)

### The Praying Coach's Daily Blueprint

1. Morning Prayer & Scripture (15–30 minutes)

Start the day not in the group chat or social media — but in silence and surrender. Flow: Thank God for waking you up. Read one chapter of scripture (start with Psalms, Proverbs, or the Gospels). Pray over your day: your mind, your mouth, your mood. "Let the morning bring me word of your unfailing love..." — Psalm 143:8 (NLT)

2. Midday Reset (2–5 minutes)

Take a break between meetings or drills. Sit. Breathe. Whisper a prayer like: "Holy Spirit, realign my focus. Let me finish strong." This resets your pace from hurried to holy.

3. Practice With Presence

Start each practice with intention — not just instruction. Say a short prayer with your staff. Cover the team spiritually before the whistle blows. Let your athletes feel God's peace even if they can't describe it yet.

4. Post-Game Prayer (Alone or with Team)

After the game, before the debrief — give it back to God. Whether it's a win or loss, don't leave the field without surrendering the result. This keeps your identity anchored in obedience, not outcome.

5. Evening Reflection & Gratitude

Before bed, ask: Where did I see God move today? Who do I need to forgive? What am I thankful for? What do I need to lay at His feet? This helps you release the weight of the day and rest in peace. "When you lie down, you will not be afraid; yes, you will lie down and your sleep will be sweet." — Proverbs 3:24 (NLT)

### The Fruit of a Prayer Lifestyle

When prayer becomes your rhythm, everything shifts:

1. You respond instead of react.
2. You stay grounded when pressure rises.
3. You lead with discernment, not ego.
4. You carry peace into every room.
5. You build legacy — not just a record.

"They will be called oaks of righteousness, a planting of the Lord for the display of his splendor."
   — Isaiah 61:3 (NLT)

### Common Distractions (and How to Overcome Them)

1. Busyness – Create margin. Protect quiet time like you do film study.

2. Guilt – God's not asking for perfection. He's asking for presence.

3. Disappointment – Don't let delays or discouragement stop you. Keep showing up.

4. Laziness – Build habit through structure. Leave your Bible where you'll see it. Set reminders.

5. Doubt – You're not "too late." God honors every step back into rhythm.

### Accountability for the Long Haul

Don't try to walk this path alone. Get a fellow coach or friend to check in weekly. Start a devotional or prayer group with staff or players. Share victories and struggles. Be vulnerable. Stay sharp. "As iron sharpens iron, so a friend sharpens a friend." — Proverbs 27:17 (NLT)

### Prayer for a Praying Lifestyle

Lord, I don't want to just coach with passion — I want to coach with purpose. Let my prayer life lead the way. Make it my rhythm, my reflex, and my refuge. Keep me disciplined. Keep me rooted. Help me lead from overflow — not burnout. Let my daily habits reflect heaven. Let prayer be my fuel and Your Spirit be my strength. In Yahshua's (Jesus') name, Amen.

### Reflection & Challenge

Is prayer a lifestyle for me — or an emergency tool?

Which of these daily rhythms do I already do well? Which ones can I grow in?

Do I lead my players into a lifestyle of prayer by example — or just instruction?

### Challenge:

Commit to one week of the Praying Coach Blueprint.

Set alarms or write it out where you can see it.

Journal how you feel each day. Then share the journey with another coach and invite them in.

# 13

## Conclusion: The Final Charge

### *The Power of a Praying Coach Is Just Beginning*

You didn't pick up this book by accident. You were called. Not just to lead athletes — but to shepherd souls. You may have started as just a coach. But through prayer, you've become a warrior, a mentor, a covering, a vessel. Your power is not in the clipboard, the whistle, or the win. Your power is in your connection to the One who never loses.

### *The Real Win Is Eternal*

The culture may praise championships. Social media may celebrate success stories. But heaven rejoices over something much greater: When one soul is touched, one player is loved, one heart is turned toward the light. Every time you pray with your team — you plant a seed. Every time you speak life — you push back darkness. Every time you lead with grace — you reflect the character of Christ. You may not always see the fruit immediately. But eternity will reveal the harvest of a faithful coach. "Well done, my good and faithful servant." — Matthew 25:23 (NLT)

### You Are Not Alone

There is a growing army of coaches — just like you — rising across schools, communities, and nations. They don't care about applause. They don't need approval. They want alignment with God. And you're part of that movement. Whether you coach youth or college, football or cheer, in rural towns or big cities — You are seen. You are needed. You are chosen.

### Your Legacy Starts Now

Your influence will live beyond the season. Beyond the players who graduate. Beyond the games you win or lose. Because a praying coach doesn't just coach games. They shape generations.

### The Final Encouragement

You may get tired — but don't give up. You may feel unseen — but God is watching. You may feel small — but your impact is eternal. And when doubt whispers, "When will I see the fruit?" God whispers back: "You were never planting for attention — you were planting for Me."

### Prayer of Release and Recommissioning

Lord, I surrender my role as a coach back to You. Thank You for choosing me to lead, teach, correct, love, and serve. Let my heart never harden. Let my words always give life. Let my example point to You. When I grow weary, remind me I'm not alone. When I feel forgotten, remind me I'm called. Help me raise up champions not just for sport — but for Your Kingdom. Let Your favor go before me. Let Your Spirit fill me. Let my legacy be faithfulness. In Yahshua's (Jesus') name, Amen.

### Final Challenge

Pass the torch.

Find three coaches in your circle — local or online — and gift them this book.

Start a movement. Build a brotherhood. Uplift a sisterhood.

Let this be the start of your own discipleship through coaching.

Because there is still time on the clock to lead in love through prayer and action.

# The Invitation to Salvation

### A Call to Surrender Your Life to Christ

If something in this book awakened your spirit, it's not by chance—it's a divine invitation. God is calling you to Himself, and the door is open.

You can begin your journey with a simple, sincere prayer:

"Lord Yahshua (Jesus), I believe You died for my sins and rose again so I could have new life. I surrender my life to You. Come into my heart, forgive me, and lead me into Your truth. Today, I choose to follow You. Amen."

If you prayed that prayer, welcome to the family of God. Heaven rejoices with you. Now walk in your purpose and power.

### Books from Kingdom Legacy Press

- The Method Man
- The Power of a Praying Man
- The Power of a Praying Athlete
- The Power of a Praying Coach
- Rooted in Goodness
- Fathers Matter

- God's Timing is Perfect Timing
- Fixing Me, Not Him
- They'll Thank You Later
- You Are Never Too Broken

**Stay Connected & Grow**

Visit www.KingdomLegacyPress.com to subscribe for devotionals, online studies, and upcoming book releases.

You can also find resources to help deepen your faith, strengthen your family, and live a life aligned with God.

Join the movement. Walk in purpose. Become the light.